CONNECTIONS
Railway Verses

Peter Burgham

First Printing: 2023

ISBN 978-1-9196018-5-4   (paperback)

Published by: Peter Burgham
                 York, England

A CIP catalogue record for this book is available from the British Library.

Website: www.burg34.com

Front Cover: York Railway Station
Back Cover: Hebden Bridge signal box

*Dedicated to my wife
and our family and friends
with love*

Connections : Railway Verses

Whilst never having been a trainspotter, I do have a great interest in and affection for the railways of Great Britain. I live in York, a city with a tremendous railway heritage, and so it is with a certain bias that my front cover shows York station. I've tried to showcase as many aspects of the railways as practical in a small volume, but there simply isn't enough space to include everything. No room even for the Eurostar, signal boxes, station buffets, freight trains, engineering, iconic routes, the HS2 saga, Beeching cuts, movies, level crossings (sorry, no 'Ode to a Level Crossing'), or quiet (huh !) coaches – maybe next time !

Each subject chosen highlights an aspect of railway life that has impacted further afield, and I have consciously used a variety of poetic styles, from free verse to limericks, to try to broaden the appeal – and there's no shortage of rhymes for those who like 'proper' poetry ! Each section has a short narrative to give a bit more historical context and depth.

The ditty on the back cover refers to one of the most significant repercussions on society made by the railways, involving timetabling in the mid-19th century. Until 1840, solar time had been used in towns and villages throughout the UK. But with variations of up to ten minutes, this led to confusion in train timetabling, and so London time was adopted. This led to its adaptation not just on the railways but in society at large, and standard time was born.

And nowadays, as the memory of the famed curly sandwich has all but disappeared, we should wish for every success in finally making the best of the opportunity we have with rail travel in the UK. But however things may turn out, let's console ourselves with the old adage that it's the journey that's the really interesting part ... even if - as we know - it can sometimes be somewhat fraught !

We are all 'connected' in one way or another to the railways in this country, so 'Connections' seemed to be my least worst option as a title ! Welcome then to this short journey on the railways. Hopefully you will have a first class experience. All aboard !

Topics

Ticket Inspectors 7
Victorians 8
Timetables 10
Seaside Resorts 12
National Railway Museum 14
Mountain Railways/Funiculars 16
Model Railways 18
Evacuees 20
Writers on Trains 22
Tunnels 24
Industrial Revolution 26
Disused Lines 28
Bridges and Viaducts 30
Railway Hotels 32
Heritage Railways 34
Miscellaneous 36

Index of Poems

Tickets Please 7
Victorians 9
Smokescreen 11
Whistle 11
The Train to Wick is Cancelled 11
Kipling at the Bingo 13
Trainspotting 15
Seeking the Music 17
Barnstaple Flyer 19
I'll Take That One 21
Train Limericks 23
No Mere Hole in the Rocks 25
The Magic of Totley Tunnel 25
Up on the Hill 27
An Alien Family Visits Theme Park Earth 29
Rhapsody in Steel 31
Afternoon Haiku with Scones and Jam 33
Semaphore Signals 35
The Half-Jostle 36
Caught Smiling on the Tube Today 37
Station Signs 38
If Musicians Ran The Railways 39
Coaching Tips 40
Arthur's Flamingo 41
Travelling Backwards 42

TICKET INSPECTORS

They've seen it all, the ticket inspectors ...

Tickets Please

the jubilant fans
    the crushed empty cans
        the young and the old
            the stories being told

the leaves on the track
    the cheeky feedback
        the crafty fare dodgers
            the grumpy old codgers

the snail-paced, the pale-faced
    the fallen asleep
        the scurriers, the worriers
            the gamers fast and deep

the cards on the table
    the volume up loud
        the fake designer label
            the party-time crowd

the sneezes and coughs
    the litter on the floor
        the pigs in their troughs
            the scrawl on the door

the wrong day of travel
    the payments declined
        the yarns they unravel
            the years left behind

VICTORIANS

The Victorians totally transformed the landscape of travel in the UK, sparking a transport revolution across the globe.

Prior to the introduction of the railway, the journey between Liverpool and Manchester had taken 12 hours by canal, 3 hours by coach; the train completed the trip in not much more than half the time of the stagecoach.

The period between 1830 and 1845 became known as 'Railway Mania' as dozens of lines were built across the country.

Source: Science and Industry Museum, Manchester.

This poem compares Victorians to magicians, and when we see the amazing things they achieved with the resources they had, it can appear to be quite miraculous ...

Victorians

The Victorians liked an illusion
they juggled the solar clock
and with exemplary extrusion
made big holes out of rock.

A puff of smoke and a tap on the wheel
in a show of prestidigitation
what came out of the hat was quite surreal -
a Rocket and a standing ovation.

The minutes vanished in a flash
in Carnforth, York and Crewe,
the stagecoach horses felt the lash
as iron ones whistled through.

From Darlington and Marston Moor
from Hull and East Kilbride
they conjured trips to Blackpool's shore
and then - for a grand finale -
        pulled white doves out of Bradshaw's Guide.

TIMETABLES

Until the introduction of train timetables in the mid-19th century the time across the UK was not standardised. Variations of up to 10 minutes could be found. This proved too confusing for timetabling, until London time was used across the railway network in 1840, leading to its adoption by all public authorities by 1855. And in 1884 GMT became the international basis for 24 hourly time zones.

Source: Network Rail

There is no perfect railway, even in Switzerland trains get cancelled. Snow, leaves, illness, mechanical troubles. It happens. Scheduling is an art form, as anyone who has actually had to try to do it will tell you.

But like everybody else, I still grumble if my train is late and I miss my connection ...

Smokescreen

The Victorians liked an illusion
And as the smoke began to clear
With dexterous suffusion
They'd made time disappear ...

Whistle

We all have a timetable
that we're destined
to keep

and even if sometimes
we feel we're knee-deep

we all make a journey
or at least scrape along

heading down the track
to find where we belong

'cos it's better to have
travelled
than never at all

so climb aboard quick
when you hear that
train whistle call.

The Train to Wick is Cancelled

And if you don't make it to Wick that day, you know there'll
always be another for that business meeting, or that cup of
tea with a friend. You are wise, you see beyond the headlines
and the mumbo jumbo. Because on the day the Great
Announcer signals the final cancellation, you know there
will be no refund available ...

SEASIDE RESORTS

The railways changed what was possible for ordinary working people, opening up routes to the British seaside. Resorts such as Blackpool, Margate, Brighton, Rhyl, Llandudno, Cleethorpes, Scarborough, Largs and Ayr flourished as people flocked from grimy industrial towns to spend their hard-earned money on relaxation and amusement.

The heyday came in the 1950s and 1960s, when regular holidays became more affordable to working people through annual paid leave. Butlin's holiday camp at Filey even had its own railway station.

With profound apologies to Rudyard Kipling for this poem !

I use my fictional town of 'Baycombe' as a generic British seaside resort. Substitute your own favourite resort when reading the verse !

Kipling at the Bingo

If you can build your castle high
Then see it swept away
If you can triumph at the bingo
And treat losing in just t'same way

If you can funnel pennies into slots
And watch them meet their doom
If you can bear to go to Baycombe
On a winter's afternoon

If you can ride life's rollercoaster
And take the spins and jolts
If you can take the world for what it is
And tolerate its faults

You'll be t'king of t'castle, my son.

NATIONAL RAILWAY MUSEUM

The National Railway Museum is in York, close to the mainline station. It tells the story of rail transport in Great Britain and beyond, and its impact on society.

It includes permanent and temporary exhibits, such as the Mallard, Stephenson's Rocket, and the Japanese bullet train, and is closely associated with the Flying Scotsman.

Since its official opening in 1975 by HRH Prince Philip, Duke of Edinburgh, it has continued to grow and diversify.
It remains a major tourist attraction.

This poem was inspired by something I saw whilst driving on York outer ring road. It was an old engine that looked very much like Stephenson's Rocket, being carried on a flatbed trailer presumably to the Museum.

Image by kind permission of National Railway Museum.

Trainspotting

It was history served on a plate, its vintage glory
signalled on the up, a much-heralded arrival,
its preservation a triumph over every rival,
a strike of the gong heard from Beattock to Adlestrop
announcing Museum as the next station stop,
where well-versed stewards will safeguard the story.

Black-blooded aristocracy on the York outer ring,
streamlined and peerless in its model design
the very definition of *X Factor* in 1829
when *Downton Abbey* was the future sought,
and the *Tay Bridge Disaster* wasn't even a thought,
its fame is its ticket to ride like a king.

The weight of antiquity on a rickety old flatbed
rolling to a timetable nationwide planned,
en route towards its ancestral stand
to join the *Mallard*, the *Bullet* and the *Flying Scotsman*
and shunt the black sheep of the railway clan
the unloved old diesels to the sidings shed.

Resplendent and dapper, its chimney iconic,
an infusion of class on a diesel-dull Tuesday,
this mythical apparition evoking a ghost play
of top hats and tails in a school-textbook scene
where crowds rushed to touch the sleek new machine
(apart from one whose brush with history was sadly ironic).

But then from magic to tragic befitting Harry Potter
came the spike in the rail, the muggledom truth,
the googled discovery of iron-clad proof,
plainly this wasn't *The Legend* in view
but the *Baycombe Belle* a lesser marque from Crewe
yet story enough for the avid trainspotter.

MOUNTAIN RAILWAYS/FUNICULARS

The mountain and funicular/cliff railways of Great Britain
are not perhaps as lauded as some of their continental
counterparts but no less interesting.

Amongst the most well-known are Snowdon, Brecon,
Cairngorms, Saltburn, Lynton & Lynmouth, Babbacombe,
Bridgnorth, with many others dotted about the country.

Gradients and track gauges vary, as does the type of
ownership, but they all share a common aim:
sustainable tourism and the appreciation of railways.

This poem reflects a fog-bound visit to the top of Snowdon,
where the author was 'seeking the music' ...

                ... somewhat in vain !

Seeking the Music

There's music in the mountains
far from the factory din
so head for the heights
with your rucksack of words
          and let the musicals begin.

The second part of my poem
will be the greatest poem of the modern day
but you'll have to take my word for it
as I've only got halfway ...

MODEL RAILWAYS

The pastime of model railways is still very popular. Building a model railway is a creative family-oriented hobby that encourages hands-on engagement, teaches patience and planning skills, and is indeed educational about railways in general.

There are many clubs and national associations, some very long-established. Annual conventions and regular contests are held.

Many celebrities have also declared their interest in the hobby and in doing so have made it -

dare one say? - cooler !

This poem evokes how engrossing and fulfilling the hobby can be, allowing people of all ages to indulge and become orchestrators of this magical world.

Barnstaple Flyer

Clasping an umber-and-cream Pullman
     restaurant car in his hand,
the hobbyist guides it smoothly onto the rails,
     couples it behind the Mallard,
or maybe today the Barnstaple Flyer.

Eagerly, he slides in the maroon
     Royal Mail carriage, flap door ready
to spring the waiting mailbag
     as it flashes by on its dutiful mission.

With finger and thumb, he airlifts
     a signal box to the other side
of the footbridge, deftly re-aligns
     the geography of houses.

Assembling his orchestra, he arranges
     a siding and a shed with precision,
calls in a black 2-6-4 engine
     shunted for repairs.

In the toot of a whistle, the baton twirled,
     he sets the tempo and direction,
brings his ensemble to concert pitch,
     the maestro of his world.

He is giant, he is king.

EVACUEES

During World War II, over 3.4 million people (mainly schoolchildren) were evacuated on government advice for safety away from towns and cities to stay with strangers usually in rural areas.

This was the biggest single movement of people ever in the UK, accomplished largely via the rail network.

Some found welcoming foster homes, but for others it was the start of a nightmare that had a lasting impact.

This poem, inspired by stories retold in my family, tries to capture the chaos of the moment in September 1939 when thousands of schoolchildren were taken to railway stations all over the country and sent away from their parents and in some cases their siblings, for an indeterminate length of time.

I'll Take That One

At the station
a bedlam of souls
exhorted to neat lines
by schoolteachers

a sea of hands
waving   drowning

gas masks
boxed and alien
a babble of voices

mothers in lines
lips quivering
hands reaching out

hands whistled away
into the smoke

down the line
the kids chatter
to the clatter
of wooden carriages
scoff their picnics
pull faces and legs
heady with the smell
of soot and oil

peering faces pressed
to windows spy a
blacked-out platform

another whistle blow

an orderly procession
into the village hall

the line-up
the hush

the bombshell

WRITERS ON TRAINS

One of the beauties of rail travel is its ability to let the passenger relax. There was a famous TV advertising jingle in the 1970s to that effect.

Unlike driving a car, on a train you can read a book, play a game on your mobile device, gaze out of the window, get up and take a walk etc.

Tables and dropdown trays are standard features that aren't just for resting your coffee on.

Little wonder then that many people enjoy writing while travelling on trains.

Here's some old-fashioned daft limericks that I wrote while enjoying a train ride or two.

Train Limericks

There once was a lady called Dolly
Whose job was to push the tea trolley
She served with a smile
As she stood in the aisle
But to think you'd get past is just folly.

       A group of old friends playing Cluedo
       Preferred it to judo and Ludo
       But what tickled the guard
       When he told them they're barred
       They were playing the game in the nuedo.

A man in a carriage at Crewe
Was looking for something to do
So he sketched a big hen
Then he sketched it again
It was a cockadoodle déjà vu.

       There was an old stoker from Stoke
       Who sold surplus coal to some bloke
       He was caught in a flash
       With his hands on the cash
       He got fired and it wasn't a joke.

There was a young porter called Short
Who gave some things far too much thought
Like, what is a skance ?
Can elephants dance ?
And is beer-mat flipping a sport ?

       A panda escaped from the zoo
       In the buffet car en route down to Looe
       He fancied a meal
       And got told here's the deal
       Please wait behind the chimp and the gnu.

A lady who sat in first class
Demanded champagne in a glass
When she got it in plastic
Her reaction was drastic
She blamed it on Brexit en masse.

TUNNELS

The tunnel boring machines being used in the 21st century are loud, heavy monsters that chew up and spit out enormous chunks of earth in timescales unimaginable to our Victorian forefathers.

There were very few if any tunnel boring machines in the 1860s. Tunnels were built essentially by hand, by teams of 'navvies' (derived from the word 'navigator') who laboured long and hard in often dangerous conditions.

It is thanks to their efforts that many difficulties were overcome, leaving us with a legacy of routes, both overground and underground, that connect places that previously would have been isolated or tortuous to reach.

These poems praise the efforts of those sterling workers.

No Mere Hole in the Rocks

The curves and slopes you cannot track
Underneath the arch pitch black
No signal from its frowning guise
No light upon its dull surprise
Echoing far in its soot-tarred box
Legacy gift from the school of hard knocks
Silently knowing, no mere hole in the rocks.

The Magic of Totley Tunnel

At Grindleford tha'll still
 Be in Derbyshire
  Reet fine it mebbe but
   As tha knows ther's only one
    County where t' sun allus shines
     And to get t' promised
      Dominion tha's no mair than
       A puff of smoke away
        Before t' saintly paradise can be
         Reached, t' magic at th'end o' tunnel
          A flash o' light delivrin' thi to godzone Yorkshire …

INDUSTRIAL REVOLUTION

Richard Arkwright and others transformed the economic landscape in the latter part of the 18th century with the introduction of machinery to perform tasks far more rapidly than could be achieved by hand. The factories and mills were born, with their attendant rules and constraints. The working week and weekends became concepts.

Life in these places was undoubtedly very hard. Some mill owners such as Titus Salt became renowned for their philanthropy and concern for the welfare of their workers, leading to significant social reforms.

The advent of the railways in the mid-19th century revolutionised the distribution of the goods and supply of raw materials, igniting the rapid expansion of places like Manchester, Leeds and Liverpool into the cities we know today.

But the gap between rich and poor became greater, leading to social unrest - sound familiar?

Up on the Hill

Up on the hill, where the air is fresher,
away from the milling crowd
and the steam-charged pressure,
like a rich merchant of old,
who'd count a success
raking in more gold
while forking out less,
in a white-washed house
looking down on the chase,
with a view that's as clean
as the breeze on your face,
how I'd love to live
a life of leisure,
up on the hill,
where the air is fresher.

DISUSED LINES

There are hundreds of former railway cuttings across the country now transformed by nature into wildlife highways.

Walking or cycling along the path of disused lines has become a very popular pastime in recent years, with some interesting re-visioning of usage.

This has been an unexpected spin-off benefit of the notorious Beeching cuts in the 1960s, when many branch lines and small stations were closed.

From railways to trailways ...

Part of the former East Coast mainline track, from York to Riccall, has been transformed into a footpath and cycleway. This incorporates a scale model Solar System Trail, with a sculpture of each planet located at the appropriate spot along the 10km trail, giving you a very visual insight into the vastness of the cosmos.

Image by kind permission of University of York.

An Alien Family Visits Theme Park Earth

You can land your spacecraft at the Transportation Centre the **Earth Ants** call 'ParknRide'. It's an easy walk to the **Sun**, where it all starts, as you kids know.

(A 'walk' is a slow fuel-efficient mode of propulsion. For increased velocity, Earth Ants also sometimes balance on mechanical devices propelled by their feelers, scattering the slower ants with odd noises.)

Then it's only a short spacehop-and-a-skip to **Mercury**, at 3 times the speed of light, the kids loved the thrill of covering 57 million kilometres in 100 Earth steps. We flew past **Venus** in no time at all. Then we went right round the **Earth** and the **Moon**, before we trekked on to **Mars**, which the Earth Ants seem very interested in, but the kids think isn't so cool.

Treknote: If you want a break, you can try the Ant sustaining fluid in a mission for voyagers in the satellite colony of 'Bishopthorpe', about halfway to **Jupiter**.

You then cross a small channel of liquid to get to **Saturn** – the Earth Ants use a curious passage over it, which in their history was built for strange metallic contraptions wrapped in white clouds.

You're at the mid-point now, 'Naburn Lock' in Ant-speak. It's nearly as far again to reach **Uranus,** where we had our sandwiches. Then it's a 15-nanosecond mechanical device ride to **Neptune**. There's some old Earth mines of unecological black fuel nearby.

Finally we reached **Pluto** – to think we've been to Pluto today and we still got back home in time for tea.

The kids liked to mimic the Ant-speak and made up a song which they called the 'Ant Chant' and sang all the way home.

> "Ey up it's reet gradely is Earth
> 'ow much d'ye reckon it's worth?"

We know Earth has got terrible ratings – only one star – but we felt right at home in this habitat they call 'Yorkshire' …

BRIDGES AND VIADUCTS

There is no finer expression of the railway line than a spectacular viaduct. We are fortunate in Britain to have a plethora of marvellous examples, many still in use, from Glenfinnan to Leaderfoot to Ribblehead to Esk Valley to Knaresborough to Cefn-Coed. Views over many accessible viaducts are often breathtaking.

Bridges too range in style and size and materials, with famous examples such as Brunel's Royal Albert Bridge at Saltash, Stephenson's Conwy Railway Bridge, and the world's oldest one still in continuous use, Skerne Bridge in Darlington.

Source: Network Rail

The poem is a eulogy for the perhaps the most famous of them all, the iconic Forth Bridge, opened in 1890. At the time it had the longest bridge spans in the world. Its style is truly impressive.

It remains one of the greatest cantilever trussed bridges, and is a UNESCO World Heritage Site.

Rhapsody in Steel

Colossal spirit of the age of Empire,
with ghosts and whistles of trains
long since spotted,

billowing and thundering
in the mesh of girders,
iron-clad dark chargers champing

through the buffeting swirl
of winds and sepia mist,
the Bridge enduring

the dour tetchy Forth,
an industrial diamond
matchless in its prime,

braw vision of the Victorian
railway man, perfectly blending
the art with the artisan,

a showcase all spick and span
before the inevitable grime,
its patched-up wounds

a bell-toll in the fog
for every worker lost,
the legend forged from

sweat & tears & myriad
paint schemes endlessly enacted,
heaving to the last wire,

engine of creation,

poetry in steel.

RAILWAY HOTELS

Prestigious hotels popped up seemingly everywhere in the Victorian heyday, and into the 20th century, with many famous people being attracted to stay, creating a certain glamorous mystique which is their legacy today.

The very names evoke the heritage:

Derby Midland - the oldest surviving railway hotel
Bradford Great Victoria - favoured haunt of celebrities
Royal York (now Principal) - a grade II listed building
Manchester Midland - where a Mr Rolls met a Mr Royce
Edinburgh Balmoral - in the heart of the Scottish capital
and the archetype - the iconic St. Pancras Renaissance
(and not forgetting the Royal Baycombe, my fictional one !)

Afternoon tea remains a favourite indulgence that can be enjoyed at virtually all the UK's historic railway hotels, often in glamorous surroundings. The Haiku format of three structured lines lends itself well to celebrating this ritual.

Afternoon Haiku with Scones and Jam

Petit-fours at three
with a pot of tea for two
always time for one

Earl Grey and Jasmine
two jazz singers of renown
hit notes to a tea

Cucumber sandwich
prawn cocktail, salmon and dill
kudos on a plate

Whether plain or fruit
oozing clotted cream and jam
fastest cake it's scone

HERITAGE RAILWAYS

The enduring popularity of heritage transport experiences is evidenced by over 200 heritage and minor railways operating across Great Britain, despite the many challenges facing them.

Mainly but not exclusively focused on steam locomotion, with much of the rolling stock original and of historic value in itself, these organisations are run by a mix of employees and volunteers and are largely self-funded. They operate under the umbrella of the Heritage Railway Association (HRA) which regulates safety aspects.

Source: Heritage Railway Association

Amongst the best-known are West Somerset Railway, Swanage Railway, North Yorkshire Moors Railway, Ffestiniog Railway, Dartmouth Steam Railway, Llangollen Railway and Keighley & Worth Valley Railway.

The poem highlights the romanticism and nostalgia inherent in the sector.

Semaphore Signals

She speaks in a welter of sound
as she builds up her speed and her glory is crowned
by a chug and a toot and a clackety-clack
as she hurtles like an Arrow straight down the track.

She speaks of the days when coal was king,
when romance was charmed from a piston ring,
her legend was sparked and the world was amazed,
as records were claimed and trails were blazed.

She speaks with her classical style,
potboiler stories for mile upon mile,
of stiff-upper-lips and spies on the run,
fleeting encounters and Will Hay-type fun.

She speaks with her semaphore of steam,
signalling green in the eye of her dream,
rolling along so stately and proud,
majestically framed in her white thunder cloud.

She speaks to us now in so many ways,
a labour of love in a sepia haze.

The Half-Jostle

The *Full Jostle* is practised in some parts of town
(Google: 'kids schoolbus anarchic scrumdown')
but in general we grown-up Brits are far too polite,
so for us it's the *Half-Jostle*, the edging forward
ever so slight.

In recent years it seems that techniques have improved
and several new skills have been duly approved:
the *Half-Step Shuffle* and the *Swinging Backpack*,
and the *Yellow Line Dance* to angle your attack.

But of course we want to keep our sport clean
so the *Full Headlock* is now no longer to be seen,
and to be more inclusive and gain old people's trust
we've authorised the pensioner's *Walking Stick Thrust*.

Final tip, as the train approaches the platform,
make sure you limber up for the gathering storm,
position those toes on the verge of the start line,
and focus your thoughts:
'that luggage rack space – it's mine !'

Caught Smiling on the Tube Today

Turns out he was a serial offender
a flasher, a beamer, a hardened message-sender
determined to prevail, a real bitter-ender
a man with a big obsession.

Arrested by the metropolitan uniformity
for his blatant anti-conformity
they pointed out the enormity
of his toothy indiscretion.

The newspapers picked up the story
and railed in terms most derogatory
claiming jail-time should be mandatory
for such a gross expression.

But when it came to his defence
his protestations were intense
on the grounds - and it did make sense -
that he was a member
of the dental profession.

Station Signs

Llanfairpwllgwyngyllgogerychwyrndrobwllllantysiliogogogoch
Welsh for beginners ... how do you say:
'May I have 2 tickets for Llanfair ... er ... Colwyn Bay?'

Brockenhurst
There's a German twin town of Brockenhurst
It's not the best but it's not the wurst ...

Matlock Bath
Matlock Bath is well renowned
It once got lost and now it's found ...

Cromford
When Prince Charles was here we pinned up a plaque
Some people say it was to cover up a crack ...

Saltaire
Our town's got a Tesco
But Saltaire's got UNESCO ...

Chesterfield
It's come to our attention - one crooked spire -
In need of a handyman who's got a giant plier ...

Dunkeld & Birnam
I've never seen them move, the woods around here,
But if ever they did, I'd be off like a deer ...

If Musicians Ran The Railways

Singalongs would be organised in each coach, led by Irish folk bands. All on-board announcements would rhyme and be sung a cappella.

Standard coaches would be themed by musical genre:
A - Acoustic, B - Blues, C - Country, J - Jazz, M - Metal etc.
Note regional variations:
for Scottish services B - Bagpipes, and in Wales H - Harp replaces Hip Hop.

A new class called 'moshpit' would be introduced -
nb standing only - familiar already to peaktime travellers -
but for moshpit, tickets would be free.

The two-tone klaxon on trains would be replaced by the guitar riff from 'Smoke on the Water'. Every Saturday night giant inflatables shaped like animals would be released into the rafters of vaulted Victorian stations.

Quiet coaches would be equipped with personal headsets playing John Cage 4'33 on continuous loop.

At Christmas, a traditional carol concert would be performed on all cross-country services queuing around Manchester Piccadilly by a mixed choir of catering staff and passengers, directed by the conductor in Santa hat.

When pulling the emergency chord, Eric Clapton would appear, god-like, and with one mighty strum bring light into any tunnel.

Cancellations would be sung by gospel choirs with hallelujahs for every bus replacement service and the world would seem a better place.

All proceeds from fares would be used to improve the services, alongside a fund in the Musicians' Union to eradicate hardship for musicians, and of course all musicians would travel free, for life, and amidst all this harmony and joy, nobody would ever need to complain.

Worth a try ? .....

Coaching Tips

Coach A

Aardvarks are rarely left
Aboard trains
Actually. There are now
Additional measures for
Aerosol-sprayers who should be forced
Afterwards to carry the can for crimes
Against carriages.
Ah and fines will also be made for
Aisle baggage. A door is never left
Ajar on a train as this is
Akin to the bad practice of
Allowing the tannoy to crackle
Ambiguous and misleading
Announcements eg offering bottled
Aorta which does regrettably
Approximate in sound to 'bottled water'.
Aquatic sports are prohibited on board. Upon
Arrival at the Oval stop which is rectangular
Assistance should be provided
At once for confused tourists especially
Australians. If no food or drink is
Available today, it's because the trolley lady's run
Away with the chef. On no account should
Axes be left on the train
Aye that's right because it's
Azure thing somebody will think
     the service is for the chop.

    Coach B

    Bans are in place for
    BB contestants
    Bcos .. Well, because ..
    BD .. Big data, big deals ..
    Bells and whistles ..
    Bf .. Bf .. I give up, I'm off to the buffet car
        (better luck in Coach E) ...

Arthur's Flamingo

(conversation with a stranger on a train)

'Is that a .. flamingo?' - not often asked on a train
And you might think it a question quite absurd,
But not to the man next to me smoothing the grain
Of his carefully crafted bird.

Filing his little sculpture with calm intent,
The commuter crowd leaving him undeterred,
A little culture on the 8:14 to Stoke-on-Trent,
He walked his talk, I grasped at every word.

He showed me some fine drawings that he'd sketched:
A stork, a nightingale and a bonny magpie.
And the magic of this day was duly etched:
A plain block of wood - he'd made it fly.

Now what could ever more gladden the heart
Than this brief encounter with the art of Art ?

Travelling Backwards

Their signals pulse strongest
in tunnels. You try to fathom

them, mimic their smile,
their nod, their stare. You

seem to know the shape of
them, these ghost-mirrors –

the set of the jaw, the confident
quiff of hair, the unwrinkled

eyes that fix you in time
across the darkened saloon,

fingers tensing
before the tell-tale blink,

the snatch of light
that triggers

the quick draw
of the mobile phone,

the sundance selfie
for the wanted poster.

ACKNOWLEDGEMENTS

Previously published in the **PAUSE AND REWIND** series of photo-poems by the same author:

Victorians   (slight variation)
Tickets Please   (slight variation)
Rhapsody in Steel   (reformatted)

Previously published in *Bird's Eye View*:

Trainspotting   (a reworking of *'Stephenson's Rocket'*)

Other Collections by the same author:

BIRD'S EYE VIEW
(anthology including many prize-winning and commended poems, recommended by New Writing North, Sept 2021)

TRIBUTE NIGHT AT THE SOCIAL
(3rd prize, Yeovil Writing Without Restrictions Competition, 2017)

WHISPER ON THE SHORE

TOUCHPOINTS

More poetry and verse and links to other creative arts can be found on:

www.burg34.com

Cover photo by kind permission of LNER. All the images in the book are based on my own photographs.

Disclaimer: There is no endorsement or criticism implied with regards anywhere, anything or anyone mentioned in this book.

The name 'Baycombe' is a fictional British seaside resort, also used in my 'Bird's Eye View' collection.